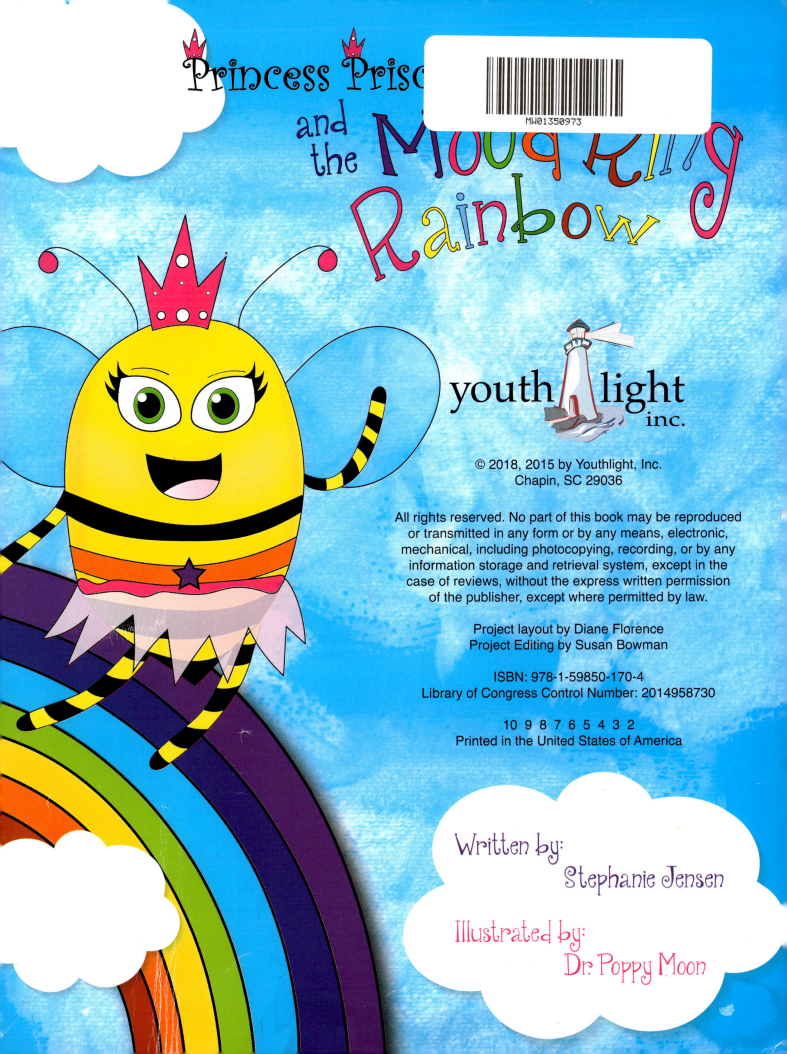

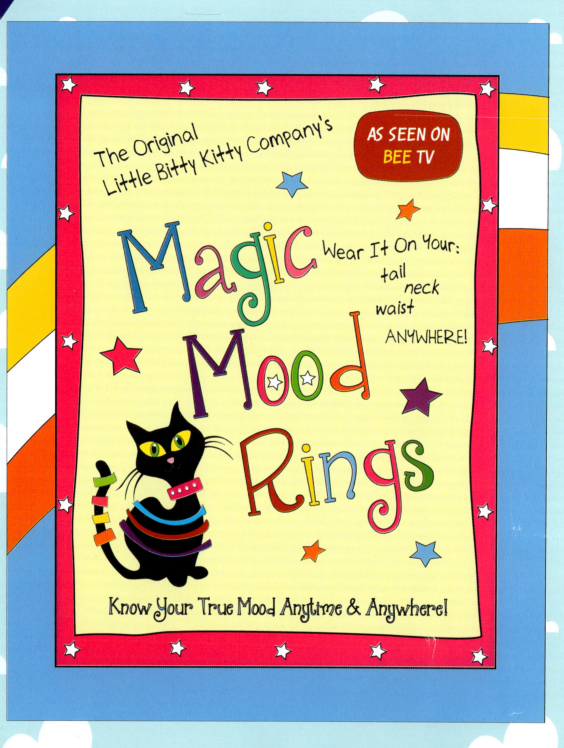

Princess Priscilla was very excited to wear her new mood ring. Now her moods would be easy to see. She thought, "No more mood guessing for me!"

She wiggled and giggled and shook until the mood ring rested on her middle. That was the right spot. One quick look in the mirror and she liked it a lot!

The ring began to change right away and a bright orange is the colored it stayed.

She loved the color and the mood was happy!

"I am

HAPPY and ORANGE is Cool!

Rose was wearing pretty new shoes. They were exactly the kind Priscilla would choose. All the bees were buzzing about Rose's new look, except Priscilla who pretended to read a book.

"Rose's new shoes are cute, don't you think?" Allie asked Priscilla. "They're the ugliest things I've ever seen!"

Priscilla looked at her ring and it had turned the color Green. She was jealous of Rose and acting mean.

She tried to think of what she had learned to do when she was in a jealous mood.

"Be honest and say something nice," was her mom's advice.

Priscilla would tell Rose she was sorry for what she said and tell her the truth instead.

"Rose, I'm sorry for what I said about your shoes. I like them very much, they are exactly like something I would choose. I was jealous they were yours and not mine and I acted mean. Will you forgive me?"

"Yes, Priscilla, I forgive you," is what Rose said. The green began to fade from the ring and Priscilla was glad.

When it was Priscilla's turn to read out loud she came to a word she'd never heard.

She felt her cheeks burn and blush and she didn't know what to think. She looked at her mood ring and it had turned pink.

Embarrassed is the mood it said. Priscilla felt embarrassed when she read.

She took a deep breath and tried one more time. With a little help she finished her turn and her cheeks didn't burn!

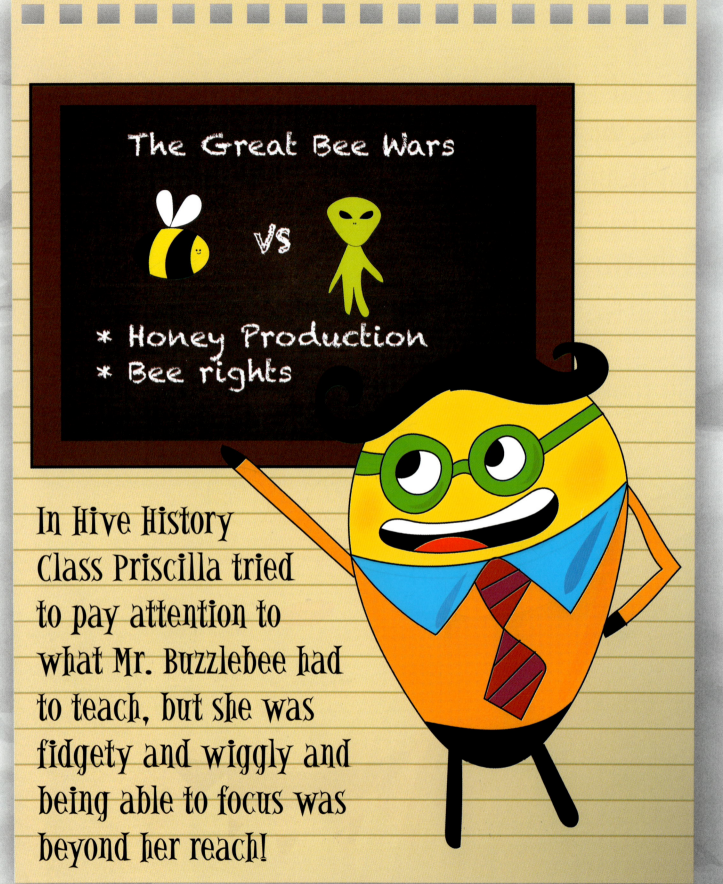

In Hive History Class Priscilla tried to pay attention to what Mr. Buzzlebee had to teach, but she was fidgety and wiggly and being able to focus was beyond her reach!

She checked the ring and it had turned a dull gray.

She was bored and didn't want that mood to stay, she didn't like the color gray!

She needed to do something to change her mood in a hurry! She just wanted the gray to go away!

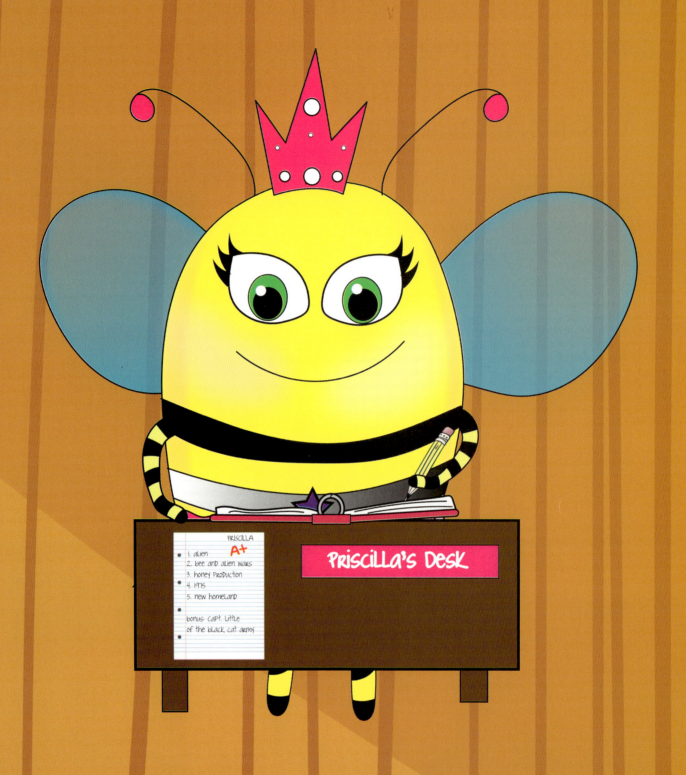

She grabbed her pencil and started to draw what Mr. Buzzlebee was talking about.

Drawing stopped her wiggles and helped her focus without a doubt. The gray quickly faded away!

Priscilla was glad she had the ring to color her mood, without it she wouldn't know what to do!

In the hall with her friends, Priscilla talked and giggled. What was her mood? She couldn't tell. She checked her ring and it turned purple; a beautiful sight!

Purple was the color for joy and the ring was right. Priscilla would stay purple as long as she could—it was a mood that felt really good!

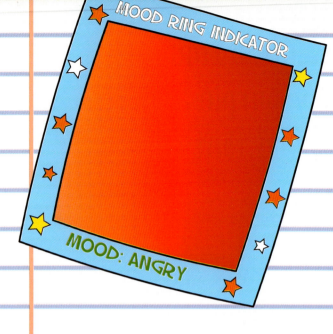

In art Priscilla asked Ms. Phoebee if she could hand out supplies, "No not today, it's not your turn."

Priscilla could feel her temperature rise. She clenched her fists and gritted her teeth; she even stomped her feet.

Like a hot fire in a fireplace the ring glowed Red just like her face!

She took three deep breaths and counted to ten.

This was always a good way to begin.

She relaxed her fingers and her anger started to fade.

Controlling her anger was the decision she made.

In math Priscilla paid attention to Ms. Bumble, but when she tried to work the problems on her own, her mind was a jumble.

She took a glance at her ring and was surprised to see all the colors swirled together, the ring didn't know what mood to choose.

It was clear Priscilla was Confused!!

She raised her hand in the air—she couldn't ignore this mood—she wouldn't dare!

She knew just what to do when she was confused—Asking for help was the skill she used!

she really missed her own dad.

She checked the ring and it had turned blue—
she was SAD—it was true

She let a tear run down her face before wiping it away. "It's ok to cry," her mom would say.

But sad was not how Priscilla would stay. She knew how to chase this gloom away.

She thought of happy times she'd had with her dad.
This helped her feel closer to him and not be so sad.

There were many colors to see—many moods of a princess bee. The ring had helped her know her mood and her mom was proud that Priscilla seemed to know what to do!

Then she buzzed around smiling, and started to sing,
"I Love Life, and Rainbows, and this Wonderful Ring!"

Princess Priscilla and the Mood Ring Rainbow

Princess Priscilla is excited to show off her new color-changing mood ring. While wearing this amazing ring around her waist, she buzzes through her day focusing on her feelings in a brand new way.

In the story, Princess Priscilla experiences many feelings and her mood ring changes colors to show each one. Each time she sees a color change, she uses one of her skills to make sure she manages her mood. At the end of the day, Priscilla uses the colors from her mood ring to draw a bright, colorful rainbow.

This story encourages self-awareness and self-management for children in a cheerful and engaging journey through the Mood Ring Rainbow with Priscilla. Children learn fundamental insights on how to name their emotions and use self-regulation strategies to manage them when needed. Princess Priscilla shows examples of positive approaches children can use when they are feeling happy, jealous, embarrassed, bored, joyful, angry, confused, or sad.

youth light inc.

P.O. Box 115 · Chapin, SC 29036
(803) 345-1070 · (800) 209-9774

www.youthlight.com

$14.95 USD

ISBN-13: 978-1-59850-170-4

9 781598 501704

Student Packet
Grades 9-12

The Bluest Eye
Toni Morrison

Activities to teach
Reading
Thinking
and
Writing

Novel Units® Teacher Guides and Student Packets

Grades 1-2
See a complete list of Grades 1-2 titles at educyberstor.com

Grades 3-4

Code 1	Code 2	Title
NU6485		Almost Starring Skinnybones
NU2722		Anastasia Krupnik
NU6450		BFG
NU6949		Basil of Baker Street
NU1882		Bear Called Paddington
NU7848	NU7856SP	Beauty
NU4164		Beezus and Ramona
NU3958		Ben and Me
NU1971	NU7015SP	Best Christmas Pageant Ever
NU6466	NU6474SP	Best School Year Ever
NU7228		Blossom Promise
NU7306	NU7314SP	Boxcar Children
NU4024		Can't You Make Them Behave, King George?
NU1904	NU7023SP	Charlie and the Chocolate Factory
NU0266	NU6302SP	Charlotte's Web
NU6523		Chocolate by Hershey: A Story About Milton S. Hershey
NU1769	NU7031SP	Chocolate Fever
NU0479	NU8259SP	Chocolate Touch
NU6477		Class Clown
NU6752		Country Artist: A Story About Beatrix Potter
NU2390		Courage of Sarah Noble
NU3966	NU8356SP	Cricket in Times Square
NU0487		Cybil War
•NU8329	NU8337SP	Danny the Champion of the World
NU3877		Ellen Tebbits
NU282X		Encyclopedia Brown
NU2560		Enormous Egg
NU2501		Fairy Rebel
NU3680		Family Under the Bridge
NU0495		Fantastic Mr. Fox
NU7888	NU7896SP	Flat Stanley
NU4431		Fourth Grade Celebrity
NU4423		Freaky Friday
NU0088	NU8224SP	Freckle Juice
NU7144	NU7152SP	Frindle
NU6008	NU6016SP	Friendship
NU668X		Grain of Rice
NU7236		Grand Escape
NU4253		Henry and the Clubhouse
NU6019		Henry Huggins
NU3869		Hundred Penny Box
NU332X		I Sailed with Columbus
NU4512		Isabelle the Itch
NU4539		J. T.
NU055X	NU4873SP	James and the Giant Peach
*NU8124	NU8132SP	Janitor's Boy
•NU837X	NU8388SP	Journey to Jo'burg
NU3311		Jumanji
NU7160	NU7179SP	Justin and the Best Biscuits in the World
NU6353		Kid in the Red Jacket
NU790X	NU7918SP	Landry News
NU2439	NU704XSP	Lion, the Witch, and the Wardrobe
NU0304	NU7058SP	Little House in the Big Woods
NU0312	NU8348SP	Little House on the Prairie
NU2846		Littles
NU0576		Long Winter
NU5896		Matilda
NU6024	NU6032SP	M. C. Higgins
NU2749	NU7066SP	Mouse and the Motorcycle
NU6973		Mystery at Loon Lake
NU6027		Not-Just-Anybody Family
NU6531		Oh, the Places He Went: A Story About Dr. Seuss
NU6132		On the Banks of Plum Creek
NU1998	NU7074SP	Owls in the Family
NU3338		Pecos Bill
NU0363		Pippi Longstocking
NU1734		Ralph S. Mouse
NU3699		Ramona and Her Father
NU6903	NU6911SP	Ramona Forever
NU4482	NU7082SP	Ramona Quimby, Age 8
NU444X		Ramona the Brave
NU4393		Ramona the Pest
NU6644	NU6652SP	Ramona's World
NU6035		Ribsy
NU1742		Runaway Ralph
NU1785	NU6310SP	Sadako and the Thousand Paper Cranes
NU0401		Sam, Bangs, and Moonshine
NU2471	NU6329SP	Sarah, Plain and Tall
NU2757		Secret Life of the Underwear Champ
NU4997		Silver
NU6040	NU6059SP	Skinny Bones
NU6558		Skylark
NU2854		Snow Treasure
NU5861		Sophie and the Sidewalk Man
NU699X		Spider Kane and the Mystery Under the May-Apple
NU7880		Stinker From Space
NU0630	NU6337SP	Stone Fox
NU671X		Stories Julian Tells
NU4520		Stuart Little
NU1750		Superfudge
NU2714	NU7090SP	Tales of a Fourth Grade Nothing
NU3346	NU8267SP	Taste of Blackberries
NU8124	NU8132SP	The Janitor's Boy
NU4105		There's a Boy in the Girls' Bathroom
NU6140		Trouble with Tuck
NU0673	NU7104SP	Trumpet of the Swan
NU1793		Velveteen Rabbit
NU7244		WANTED…Mud Blossom
NU3885		What's the Big Idea, Ben Franklin?
NU0894	NU7112SP	Whipping Boy
NU3818		Who's that Stepping on Plymouth Rock?
NU7864	NU7872SP	Wings
NU3702		Wish Giver
NU7764	NU7772SP	Yang the Youngest and His Terrible Ear

Grades 5-6

Code 1	Code 2	Title
NU3451		Abel's Island
NU6590		Alan and Naomi
NU0436		Babe the Gallant Pig
NU5621	NU563XSP	Ballad of Lucy Whipple
NU5559	NU5567SP	Barn
NU7252		Bearstone
NU5575	NU5583SP	Belle Prater's Boy
NU7063	NU7071SP	Because of Winn-Dixie
NU7899		Big Wander
NU8399	NU8771SP	Bigger
NU2862		Black Pearl
NU0940		Black Stallion
NU6957		Bodies in the Bessledorf Hotel
NU7902		Boggart
•NU8299	NU8302SP	Book of Three
NU069X		Borrowers
NU248X	NU4881SP	Bridge to Terabithia
NU0452		Brighty of the Grand Canyon
NU7910		Bristle Face
NU7260		Bronze Bow
NU6482	NU6490SP	Bud, Not Buddy
NU8984	NU8992SP	Bull Run
NU2005	NU7120SP	Bunnicula
NU8100	NU8119SP	By the Great Horn Spoon
NU2315		Cabin Faced West
NU2552		Caddie Woodlawn
NU7279		Canyon Winter
NU3710	NU8305SP	Castle in the Attic
NU2870		Cat Ate My Gymsuit
NU7929	NU7937SP	Catherine, Called Birdy
NU5888		Charley Skedaddle
NU7945		Charlie Pippin
NU7101	NU711XSP	Chasing Redbird
NU6418		Click! A Story About George Eastman
NU0967		Come Sing, Jimmy Jo
NU6701		Cracker Jackson
NU6822	NU6830SP	Crash
NU5729	NU5737SP	Crazy Horse Electric Game
NU7953	NU7961SP	Crazy Lady!
NU7287		Daphne's Book
NU2579	NU7139SP	Dear Mr. Henshaw
NU797X		Dear Napoleon, I Know You're Dead, but …
NU6965		Dew Drop Dead
NU6849	NU6857SP	Devil's Arithmetic
NU2889	NU5241SP	Door in the Wall
NU5004	NU8240SP	Egypt Game
NU6261	NU627XSP	Ella Enchanted
NU6515		Eternal Spring of Mr. Ito
NU7608	NU7616SP	Everything on a Waffle
NU 7295		Face on the Milk Carton
NU6612		Facts and Fictions of Minna Pratt
NU1890		Fighting Ground
NU6655		Fledgling
NU8208	NU881XSP	Flip Flop Girl
NU2838		Forgotten Door
NU6582		Friedrich
NU2269	NU7147SP	From the Mixed-Up Files of Mrs. Basil E. Frankweiler
NU7365	NU7373SP	Girl Who Owned a City
NU0762		Gentle Ben
NU6159		Golden Goblet
NU458X		Great Brain
NU6736		Gruel and Unusual Punishment
NU3494		Harriet the Spy
NU6547	NU6555SP	Harry Potter and the Chamber of Secrets
NU6563	NU6571SP	Harry Potter and the Prisoner of Azkaban
NU6067	NU6075SP	Harry Potter and the Sorcerer's Stone
•NU8353	NU8361SP	Homeless Bird
NU2897		Homer Price
NU0789		Horse in the Attic
NU2048	NU7155SP	How to Eat Fried Worms
NU1807		Hundred Dresses
NU1815		I, Houdini Autobiography of a Hamster
NU3443	NU833XSP	In the Year of the Boar and Jackie Robinson
NU2250	NU6930SP	Indian in the Cupboard
NU2528	NU489XSP	Island of the Blue Dolphins
NU6647		Jar of Dreams
NU2382		Jelly Belly
NU4709		Jennifer, Hecate, Macbeth, William McKinley, and Me, Elizabeth
NU8402	NU878XSP	Jeremy Thatcher, Dragon Hatcher
NU7988		Jericho's Journey
NU7309		Jim Ugly
NU7403	NU7411SP	Joey Pigza Swallowed the Key
NU7624	NU7632SP	Land
NU6434		Leaves in October
NU6604		Let the Circle Be Unbroken
NU8429	NU8801SP	Letters from Rifka
NU644X	NU6458SP	Lily's Crossing
NU6288	NU6296SP	Long Way From Chicago
NU5012		Lottery Rose
*NU8140	NU8159SP	Lupita Mañana
NU5020		Lyddie
NU3486	NU6043SP	Maniac Magee
NU6426		Mark T-W-A-I-N! A Story About Samuel Clemens
NU6671		Midnight Fox
NU6620		Midnight Horse
NU7007		Missing Gator of Gumbo Limbo
NU590X		Missing May
NU7317		Monkey Island
NU7325		Moonshiner's Son
NU1777	NU7163SP	Mr. Popper's Penguins
NU2765		Mr. Revere and I
NU7333		My Daniel
NU6566		Mystery of the Cupboard
NU654X		Night of the Twisters
NU2544	NU6051SP	Number the Stars
NU0819	NU7535SP	Old Yeller
NU3354		On My Honor
NU1076		One-Eyed Cat
NU1939		Otis Spofford
NU2900		Phantom Tollbooth
NU0592		Phillip Hall likes me. I reckon maybe.
•NU8418	NU8426SP	Pictures of Hollis Woods
NU0824	NU8275SP	Pinballs
NU637X		Pocketful of Goobers: A Story About George Washington Carver
NU5680	NU5699SP	Poppy
NU8410	NU8798SP	Question of Trust
NU0606		Rabbit Hill
NU5918		Rachel Carson: Pioneer of Ecology
NU5761	NU577XSP	Racing the Sun
NU0835		Rascal
NU7341		Red Cap
NU8003		Rescue Josh McGuire
NU2323		Return of the Indian
NU0851	NU525XSP	Roll of Thunder, Hear My Cry
NU6167		Sandra Day O'Connor: Justice For All
NU735X		Search For Delicious
NU0622	NU5268SP	Secret Garden
NU203X		Secret of the Indian
NU5926		Shades of Gray
NU4245	NU606XSP	Shiloh
NU692X	NU6938SP	Shiloh Season
NU2919		Sing Down the Moon
NU7705	NU7713SP	Single Shard
NU7489	NU7497SP	Slake's Limbo
NU6962	NU6970SP	Something Upstairs
NU9026	NU9034SP	Sparrow Hawk Red
*NU8183	NU8191SP	Stargirl
NU6083	NU6091SP	Stranded
NU5934		Strider
NU0657		Summer of the Monkeys
NU1149	NU8313SP	Summer of the Swans
•NU8434	NU8442SP	Tiger Rising
NU6698		There's a Bat in Bunk Five
NU7368		There's a Girl in My Hammerlock
NU6728		Thunder Rolling in the Mountains
NU4350		Trouble River
NU4792	NU8291SP	True Confessions of Charlotte Doyle
NU251X	NU4903SP	Tuck Everlasting
NU9042	NU9050SP	Under the Blood Red Sun
NU6574		Upstairs Room
NU9352	NU9360SP	View From Saturday
NU5039		Voyage of the Frog
*NU8221	NU823XSP	Wanderer
NU5942		War Comes to Willy Freeman

SP indicates Student Packet for this title.   * Fall 2003 title   • Spring 2004 title

Please contact us if you do not see the title you are looking for. We are always adding new titles.

www.educyberstor.com